Compositions
for Piano

Matthew Leigh EMBLETON (b1978)

Compositions for Piano

Acknowledgments

Thanks to Hong Guo for your collaboration, feedback, support, encouragement, friendship, and your fantastic recordings.

Thanks to the special people in my life who have supported and encouraged me in my work. Thank you for believing in me. You know who you are.

Op 01 Journey in d-minor

01 Introduction, *piano con affetto*

02 The Pursuit, *con affetto e un poco agitato*

03 Looking Skyward, *con larghezza*

Op 02 Nocturnes in d-minor and e-minor

01 Nocturne in d-minor, *piano molto e cantabile*

21
25
29
33

02 Nocturne in e-minor, *piano molto e cantabile*

37
41
45
49

Op 03 From Depth in a-minor

Piano molto e penseroso

21
25
29
33
37

Op 04 Nocturnes in f-minor and g-minor

01 Nocturne in f-minor, *piano molto e cantabile*

02 Nocturne in g-minor (Version 1), *piano molto e cantabile*

33
37
41
45
49

02 Nocturne in g-minor (Version 2), *piano molto e cantabile*

37
41
45
49

Op 05 Small Floating Crafts in c-minor

01 Introduction, *con rubato e improvvisazione*

02 Interlude, *con rubato e improvvisazione*

03 Conclusion, *con rubato e improvvisazione*

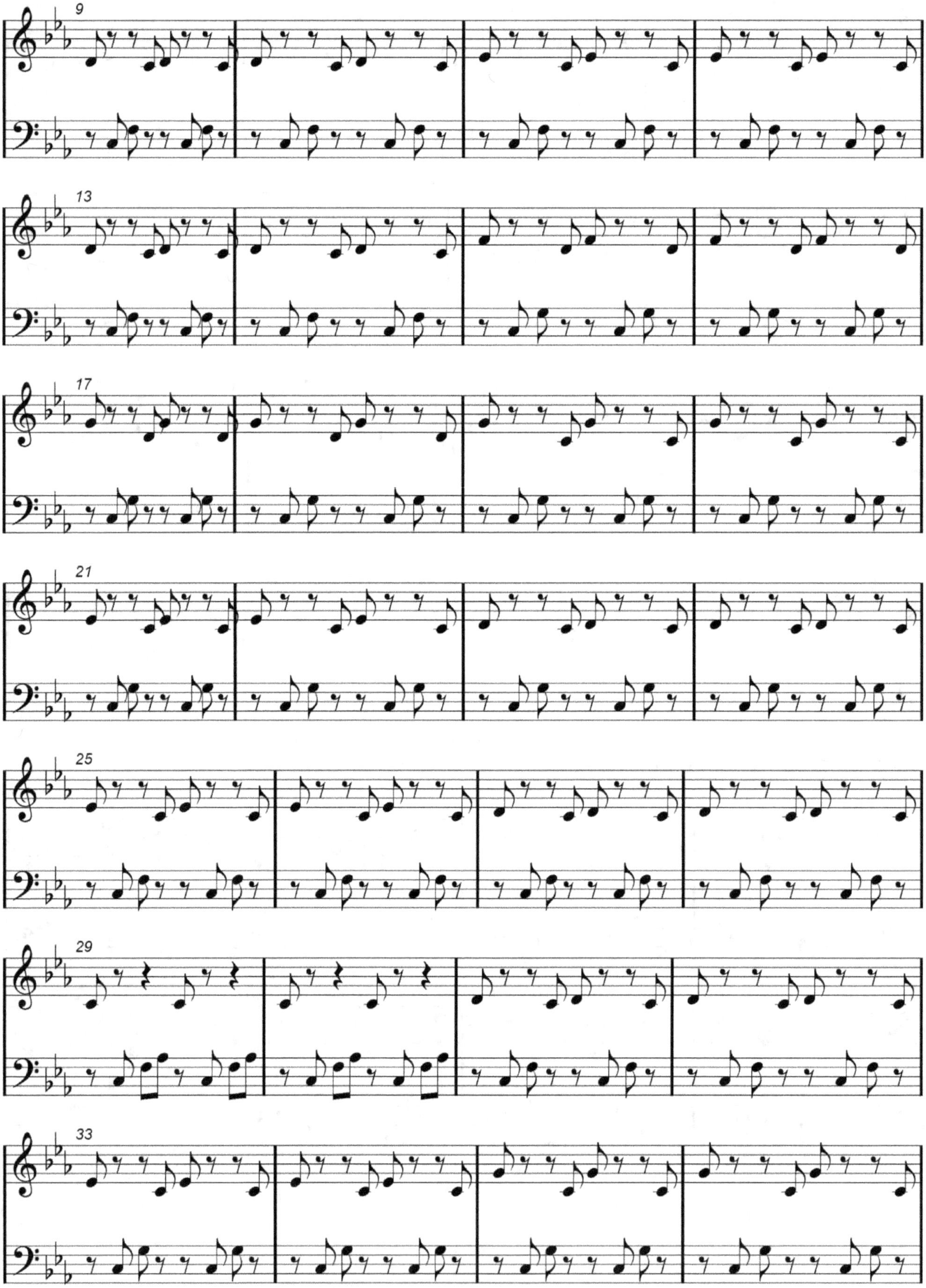
9
13
17
21
25
29
33

37
41

Op 06 Journey in a-minor

01 Arpeggiata, *adagio andante e piano*

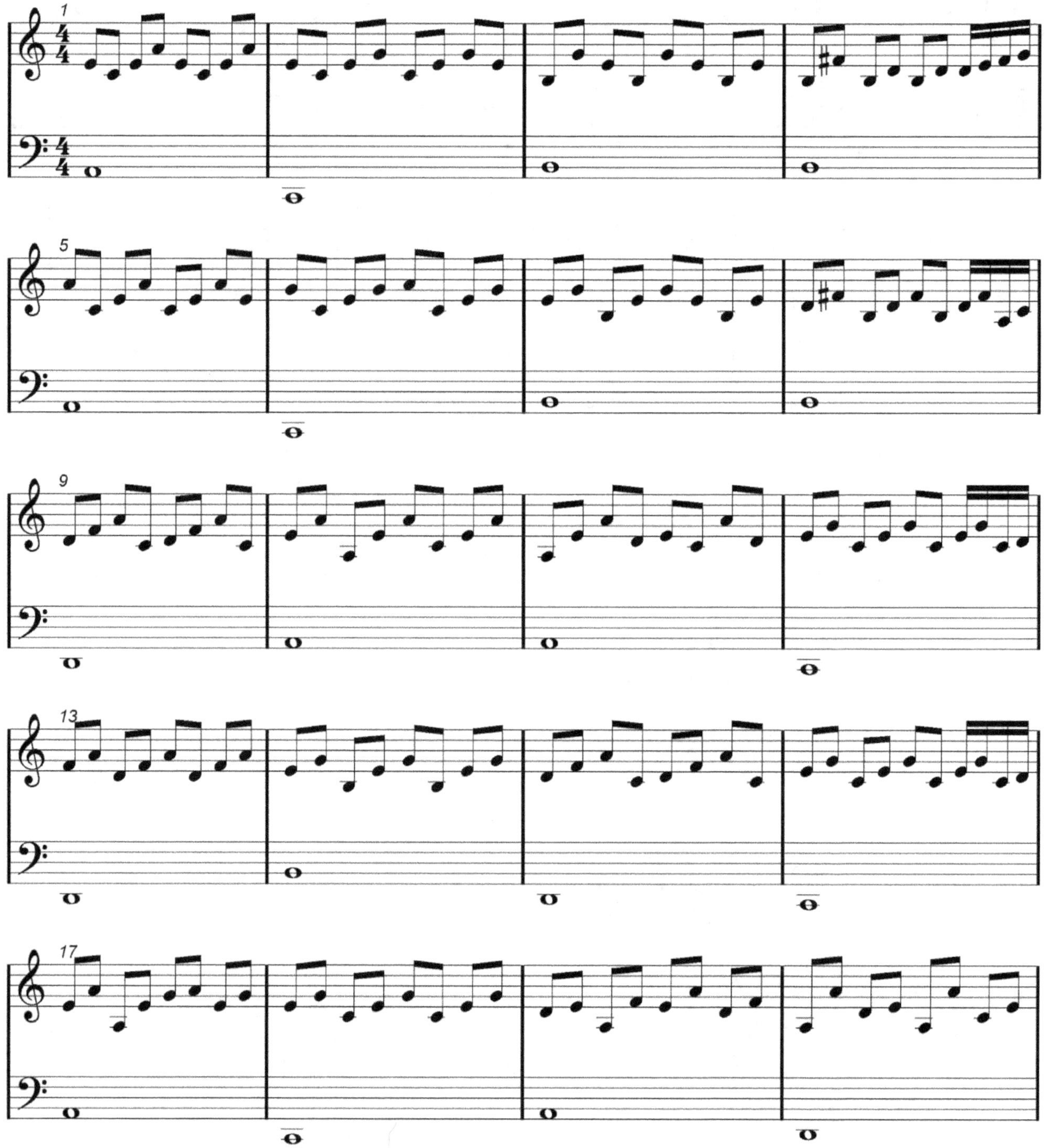

02 Cloud Level (Version 1), *piano molto e penseroso*

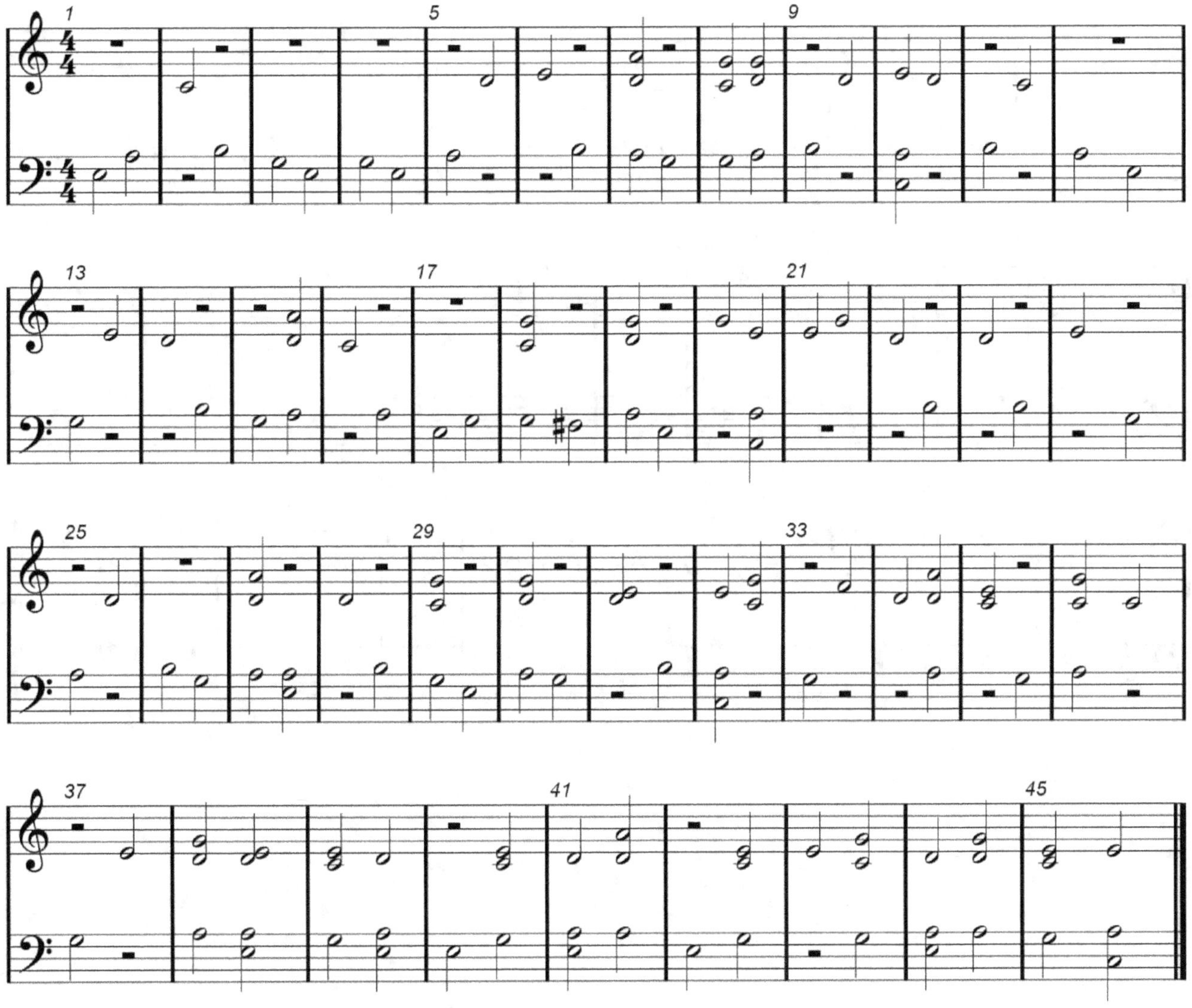

02 Cloud Level (Version 2), *piano molto e penseroso*

03 Eternal Recurrence (Version 1), *piano molto con affetuoso*

03 Eternal Recurrence (Version 2), *piano molto con affetuoso*

Op 07 Journey in c-minor

01 Introduction, *andante*

25
29
33
37
41
45
49

02 Interlude, *adagio*

03 Conclusion, *allegro*

25
29
33
37
41
45
49
53

Op 08 Nocturne in c-minor

Piano molto e cantabile

33
37
41
45
49
53
57

61
65
69
73
77
81
85
89

93
97
101
105
109
113

Op 09 Tasmanian Lake d-minor

Piano molto e penseroso

33
37
41
45
49

Op 10 Extransience in d-minor

Affrettando con poco agitato

25

Op 11 Victoria Park, December 2005 in e-minor (Version 1)

Piano molto e penseroso

Op 11 Victoria Park, December 2005 in e-minor (Version 2)

Piano molto e penseroso

Op 12 Late Night Sky in g-minor

Piano molto e penseroso

33
37
41
45

Op 13 Introduction in g-minor

Piano molto e cantabile

37
41
45
49

www.ingramcontent.com/pod-product-compliance
Lightning Source LLC
Chambersburg PA
CBHW051426070526
44584CB00023B/3600